Theodore Marburg

The War with Spain

and The Venezuelan Dispute

Theodore Marburg

The War with Spain
and The Venezuelan Dispute

ISBN/EAN: 9783337234652

Printed in Europe, USA, Canada, Australia, Japan

Cover: Foto ©ninafisch / pixelio.de

More available books at **www.hansebooks.com**

POLITICAL PAPERS.

I. THE WAR WITH SPAIN.

II. THE VENEZUELAN DISPUTE.

BY

THEODORE MARBURG.

—————

Reprinted from *The Baltimore American.*

—————

BALTIMORE:
JOHN MURPHY & CO.
1898.

With the writer's Compliments.

POLITICAL PAPERS.

I. THE WAR WITH SPAIN.
II. THE VENEZUELAN DISPUTE.

BY

THEODORE MARBURG.

Reprinted from *The Baltimore American*.

BALTIMORE:
JOHN MURPHY & CO.
1898.

I.

THE WAR WITH SPAIN.

CONTENTS.

THE WAR WITH SPAIN.[1]

[May 1, 2, 8, 1898.]

I.

Intervention—The Law and the Practice— America Must Act Alone.

THE past few months have witnessed a con-
flict of emotions in the breast of the people.
A traditional policy and a wholesome horror of
war have been drawing them in one direction,
whilst indignation at inhuman acts impelled
them in another. Those who felt the justice of
America's position and at the same time valued
the President's noble attempt to enforce that
position without resort to war, realized that to

5

give utterance to their thoughts could only serve to encourage the war spirit and further hamper the President. Now that war has begun, it is important to examine candidly the principles involved.

The assertion most commonly heard is that we have no right to interfere in the internal affairs of another nation.

A fundamental rule of international law· is that the independence of a state must be respected. Its laws must be presumed to be fit and their execution just, and the state must be allowed to accomplish the fulfillment of its own destiny free from outside interference.

Few writers on international law have failed, however, to recognize exceptions to this rule, and some of the greatest among them include among these exceptions interference on grounds of humanity.

HEFTER recognizes it, and VATTEL says, " If the prince, by attacking the fundamental laws of the country, gives his people legitimate ground for resistance, if tyranny becomes insupportable and rouses the nation to rebellion, any power has a right to succor the oppressed people if they solicit its aid."

Prof. ARNTZ is of the opinion that interference is justified "when a government, even though acting quite within the limits of its sovereignty, violates the laws of humanity, either by measures hostile to the interests of other states, or by excessive injustice or cruelty which seriously attack our morals and our civilization."

"The right of intervention must be recognized because no matter how much the rights of sovereignty and of independence are to be respected, there is one thing even more entitled to respect and that is the right of humanity and of human society, which must not be outraged."

WOOLSEY asserts that interference is justified when crimes are committed by a government against its subjects.

Acceptance of such a principle may, of course, lead to abuses, but CALVO very properly remarks that a principle must be judged by its logical and common results, and not by possible abuses to which it may lead.

HALL states "that interference for the purpose of checking gross tyranny or for helping the efforts of a people to free itself is very commonly regarded without disfavor."

These opinions are cited not to prove that intervention on grounds of humanity is authorized by international law; many writers, among them a majority of the Italian school, reject it. The opinions are cited simply to show that the question is, at least, an open one. A just estimate would probably be that international law has not yet been developed to a sufficient extent to cover all cases of international action and that, furthermore, it has its natural and inherent limitations due to the fact that it lacks a punitive sanction.

Behind the law within the state are the police

and the whole military power of the state. Behind international law there is nothing to enforce its decrees except war. In intervening in behalf of an oppressed people the state is probably no longer moving in the sphere of international law, but must justify its acts by an appeal to the common interests of humanity or high state policy.

There are but few occasions which justify the individual in violating the wonderful and comprehensive system of law prevailing within the state. There are many occasions when the people acting in their national capacity must step outside the limits of the circumscribed body of rules called international law.

If respect for international law had proved the ruling influence with her government, France would not have aided America, and the accomplishment of American liberty would have been postponed, if not actually defeated.

If in 1827 the powers had obeyed the in-

junctions of international law, Greece would
not have been freed.

If in 1859 Louis Napoleon had felt that the
observance of international law was the highest
duty of the state, he would not have marched
into Italy to drive out the Austrian and bring
to a successful issue the noble aspirations of
Cavour and Victor Emmanuel for Italy's unity
and independence.

Actual practice shows numerous instances of
interference in the internal affairs of a nation.
The idea prevailing in former times that the
stranger was an enemy has been rapidly break-
ing down under the strides of commerce, travel
and frequent communication, and the tendency
to find kinship amongst men has as steadily
grown.   We no longer look with unconcern on
acts of oppression, no matter what the blood,
nationality or religion of the oppressed people
may be.

Most intervention has been founded on policy,
but occasionally it bears the stamp of disinter-

ested action. This is largely true, for example, of the episode of NAVARINO, an event of the Grecian struggle for independence already referred to. The barbarity with which the Turk conducted the war, pillaging, murdering and carrying off the Greeks into slavery, aroused Europe. England, France and Russia sent ships to patrol the Grecian islands and coast to prevent this, and a collision with the Turkish fleet, in October, 1827, resulted in the annihilation of the latter. Greece had then belonged to Turkey for nearly four centuries, the occupation of the Morea by Venice for a time excepted, so that this act was armed intervention in the internal affairs of Turkey. The grounds on which it was justified were: humanity, request of one of the parties, and the propriety of putting a stop to piracy and anarchy.

It differs from our intervention in Cuba in that it was the joint act of several European powers, but in this connection there is this to be considered. A little over two years ago we flung at the head of the world's great colonizer and civilizer a missive which told her that we were the arbiters on this continent, and that a policy born of the necessities of our early days was still adhered to. That policy forbids a European nation to interfere outside the sphere of her own possessions here (are not our own obligations all the heavier on this account?) and it would likewise make it difficult for us to invite any European nation to co-operate in the present armed intervention.

The desire to act more in conformance with the practice of nations with respect to intervention might next lead us to seek the co-operation of some of the American countries.

When European governments co-operate, it means the co-operation of equals. An alliance of the United States with any other American government or group of governments would not be such. Without any desire to disparage other American countries, it may be safely asserted that our power is so preponderant here, there are so many ways in which we could secure allies and influence their action, that the moral force of such an alliance would be lacking. Co-operation with other American powers would be more or less empty form, a simple reflection of European methods without their significance. It is, then, fitting that with respect to foreign questions generally we should act alone.

In the solution of this particular question, what American countries are there whose co-operation we might hope to secure? Canada is not an independent American government, whilst the balance of the powers in the western world, with the exception of the few settlements in the Guianas, are of Spanish and Portuguese origin, and could hardly be counted upon to co-operate with us in actual war against the mother country and a closely affiliated country. Logically, then, it is the United States alone that can intervene in Cuba.

II.

*Oppression Flagrant and Persistent— Ultimate
Destiny of Cuba—Just Retribution
for Spain.*

It remains to consider whether intervention
at this time is justified. The oppression which
warrants intervention in the internal affairs
of a state should be flagrant and persistent.
Many people in America and elsewhere believe
that the violation of the laws of humanity and
justice has been flagrant and persistent in Cuba.
There has been not one revolution nor short-
lived oppression which we might patiently
wait for Spain to correct, but continuous oppression for the greater part of the present
century and repeated protests in the form of
rebellion put down in a bloody manner.

The century is drawing to a close, and we
see the sense of injustice and oppression in the
Cuban as keen as ever and an attempt on the
part of Spain to reassert its authority the most

bloody and disastrous of all in the history of the island.

Whilst England has lost only one of her colonies, and great regions of the world are to-day content to remain under her flag, Spain has lost all the colonies that were strong enough to resist her power. A few islands, readily accessible and easily overrun with troops, are all that remain of her former magnificent colonial empire. Her unjust government, plunder of the people by officials, and over-taxation for the benefit of the home country have done this. This fact alone constitutes a serious arraignment of Spain's attitude in the modern world.

Cuba is so close to our shores that the long story of its wrongs has been forced upon our attention. The cry of distress which has gone up from the island so often during the century has more than once aroused the sympathy of our people. We have, indeed, been patient. If the Spanish character were different, if we

could be led to believe that Spain would be
just to Cuba in the future, we might, even at
this late day, have refrained from armed intervention, but such hope is belied by the history
of the island during the century.

The vital consideration is that the most
liberal government which the Spaniard could
grant the Cuban would not bring with it a
permanent solution of the Cuban question. It
is generally admitted that with her present
population Cuba is unfit for self-government.
This means that she must be governed from
outside, and if she remains under the Spanish
flag, it means that after an attempt at autonomy
the cruel and greedy hand of Spain will again
be found at her throat and in her pocket.
That which we have just witnessed is, then,
to be repeated. The American people have
arrived at the just conclusion that no permanent solution of the Cuban question can be
reached without turning out the Spaniard, and
they feel that it is time to act. Few deceive

themselves as to the ultimate destiny of Cuba. When we turn the present government out, the logic of events will bring us the island. We of course propose to let the inhabitants decide for themselves and try to work out their own destiny, but every thing points to the conclusion that the insecurity of life and property under self-government will in time lead them to apply for admission to the Union. Once under stable and just rule, immigration there from Anglo-Saxon countries should ultimately give a sufficient basis for sound local government.

If the unhappy island can realize in no other way the very reasonable wish for enlightened and humane government in this advanced age, is not our course proper? The world knows very well that it was not the desire to add Cuba to our territory which led to war, but if the Cuban question can be solved in no other way than by action which will ultimately bring the island to us, we should not hesitate

2

to assume the full responsibility of such action. It is best to face such an issue squarely and frankly. If we are right, it matters not whether certain of the Powers approve of our course or not; the situation at home is too delicate for them to do more than enter a diplomatic protest. It will be difficult to collect an indemnity from a country already bankrupt, and the war, which the dictates of humanity have led us to undertake, will cost us a round sum, so that we cannot be charged with acquiring the island gratuitously.

As for Spain, leave out of consideration all previous rebellions in Cuba, even all her other deeds in the present campaign of three years, and consider the sole fact of her having penned up several hundred thousand non-combatants, preventing them from earning a living, and then failing to supply them with the necessaries of life until one-half of the whole number perished. Is not the loss of Cuba a just retribution for such an act?

III.

Right of Higher Civilization.

Another important consideration is that of
the higher civilization supplanting the lower.

When the white man came to America there
were about 500,000 Indians in what now constitutes the United States. To-day there still
remain 225,000. We have then brushed aside
275,000 Indians, and in place of them have
this population of 70,000,000 of what we regard as the highest type of modern man. The
fact that the Indian, who was tolerably prolific,
did not number more than 500,000 after all
the centuries he must have lived here, indicates
a formidable struggle against nature, a struggle
against cold, famine, disease and loss of life
through internecine war; in other words, a
great sum of human misery which we have
been quite justified in brushing aside and supplanting with the peace and comparative con-
tentment and high pursuits which prevail over
the continent.

The question presented by Cuba differs only in degree. The Spaniard and his American descendant are very much the same people they were several centuries ago. What are the Spanish countries of South America, what is Spain itself doing in all the walks of life which make for progress? In previous centuries Spain has done a splendid and useful work in the western world, but she has failed to keep abreast of the world in moral and intellectual progress, and must pay the penalty. The principle that the higher civilization is justified in supplanting the lower is a dangerous one to admit, because of every nation regarding its own type as the highest, but there are certain broad facts which must force the impartial observer to admit the superiority of our own race, the Anglo-Saxon, in the qualities that contribute to human advance. At any rate, we hold to the opinion that we have done more than any other race to conquer the world for civilization in the past few centuries, and we will probably go on holding to this opinion and go on with our conquests.

If we believe that there is a distinct purpose in all that is about us and in our own
presence here, we cannot escape the conclusion
that man's express duty is the uplifting of
man. The duty to improve and elevate him-
self and his fellows thus becomes an end in
itself and a justification of life. Every rational
human being, no matter how humble his station
in life, has the power to help or hinder this
process. He is influenced principally by his
environment, made up of the national character
and tendencies, and a nation in its collective
capacity directs the process. Any nation which
blocks the way of human progress must expect
to be brushed aside by more powerful and
vigorous blood.

IV.

Wisdom of Our Course.

Is the step we have taken wise?

The first concern of a government is the
welfare of its own people, and if these people

are an enlightened, a moral, and a progressive people, the world's work is best furthered by their healthy growth. If intervention in Cuba will seriously interfere with such growth here, it must be condemned.

When the Louisiana territory, extending to the headwaters of the Mississippi and west to the Rocky Mountains, was acquired in 1803, few could foresee the portentous consequences of the act. It is now apparent that without it we would not have seized what then became a contiguous territory, California, nor made a successful claim to Oregon, and unless all this had been acquired we would have been confronted with the possibility of a rival power on the Continent, involving a standing army, extensive lines of fortification, and an occasional war.

The electric telegraph and steam navigation, the handmaids of foreign trade, are of such recent origin (within the memory of living men), that trade between the nations must be in its infancy. If this is so, the future will witness a great development of wealth along the seacoast, important cities, expensive harbors, and approaches, and with them a growth in naval power. The possession of the West Indies may then acquire an importance resembling that of the Louisiana Territory.

Presuming that our institutions are lasting, the position of power which the future will bring, must some day draw the West Indies to us. We must expect a renewal of the forward movement which led to our overrunning and acquiring Texas. The planting of its outposts in a constantly widening circle on the part of a vigorous and healthy race, is one of the most familiar processes of history. Such a matter need give the living generation but little concern as time is an element in working out such questions. When the movement of races or the history of nations is under consideration, a century or so is a short period ; but to acquire the largest and richest of the Indies now may make our inevitable task lighter in the future. When we have owned Cuba for half a century it will be a simpler matter to persuade some European government, particularly if it is seeking our moral or active support at the moment, to release or sell to us some other of the islands.

Our first President laid down for us a policy of non-interference and freedom from alliances in Europe. Soon afterward came the enunciation of the Monroe Doctrine which meant that we regarded the growth of European influence on this continent as a menace to our liberties. In our weakness we could not afford to meddle in the disputes of Europe and could not afford to have a European government constitute itself a too powerful neighbor on our own continent. This policy was next extended to include non-intervention by us in the affairs of American countries as well.

We have here a creditable perception of the needs of the young state. But that state expands in territory, in numbers, in knowledge,

and in wealth, and that which was fitting in its
youth and unripeness, hampers and dwarfs and
stifles it in its manhood. Itself subject to the
belittling influence of a discussion revolving in
a narrow circle around the tariff and finance,
it beholds kindred races playing such part
in the world's affairs that questions from all
quarters of the globe are daily knocking at
their doors for solution ; it recognizes the in-
spiring influence of such larger part ; the spirit
and moral motive and power are there, and
the nation presently moves to its proper place
among its fellows.

Only overcrowded countries can colonize
successfully. Others send their merchants
abroad, but these are not true colonizers
because only numbers and the men who labor
with their hands can colonize. The self-seeking of the colonist has spread civilization, and
nothing but self-seeking will carry on this
work. America, which is not in a position to
colonize at a distance, cannot at present take

part in the work, but it can throw its influence in favor of the best races engaged in it. It can play another role, too, an important and noble one, and play it the more successfully because it is not under any pressure to acquire territory at a distance, and its action will, therefore, be recognized as disinterested. It is the role of the arbiter who proclaims that justice shall be done, and who is powerful enough to see that justice is done. May it not happen that we can throw our weight on the side of justice abroad without interfering with home progress? Might not such a course even serve to distinctly further home progress? A great fillip would be given the national spirit through awakening the higher instincts of the people and fostering a sense of unity of purpose and proper national pride. No one denies that these were tremendous quickening factors in Germany after the Franco-Prussian war, starting her on her career of prosperity and power.

Such things afford a striking example of how that which is regarded as unreal and intangible may become of the highest practical value. Local questions which are so slow of solution now might find a solution in the new attitude of the public mind. If it succeeded in bringing a different class of men into politics the splendid machinery of our government would be made to show what it can do. There is evidence in many directions that, whilst we have made such marked progress in intelligence and wealth, the moral sense of the people has grown, too. If our politics are debased, it is not because the mass of the people are debased. In the course of the world's history it has generally been the minority that has ruled. When history was great, it was a minority of great men who made it. When an age appears degenerate, it is often because a minority of inferior men rule it, the majority remaining apathetic. A minority of the unscrupulous and active may govern a majority of honest and indifferent. Under American institutions elective bodies should really represent the best that is in the community. They ought, at least, to represent something above the average. What often actually takes place is that they do not even represent the average, but represent a minority of the worst. The reference above is to the solution of questions such as this.

In the next place, the gain in diplomatic prestige, which would follow such participation in the world's affairs, would help the country's commerce. Growth of political power is usually followed by a sharp rise in commercial importance.

In other words, whilst a moral and a progressive nation serves the world best by regarding its own interests first, and thus strengthening and developing itself, the field of an enlightened self-interest is wide enough to include discreet action abroad in the interest of humanity.

We have abundance of land and a condition

of politics within the country which pronounces against any further extension of territory until certain pressing questions are solved. The mass of the people will recognize this as the proper policy to be pursued under ordinary circumstances, but it will not prevent them from dealing like men with an exceptional condition.

In brief: Spanish rule in Cuba has caused much human misery to which it is the duty of the United States to put a stop; this can only be done by her ultimately acquiring the island since no other solution of the question would be permanent; the loss of the island to Spain is but a just retribution for inhuman acts; its ultimate acquisition by the United States may be an act of high state policy.

II.

THE VENEZUELAN DISPUTE.

THE VENEZUELAN DISPUTE.

[Reprinted from *Baltimore American* of Dec. 22, 1895.]

War and the Military System.

WHEN the cause of justice calls for war, commercial interests should never be allowed to block the way. Aside from the question of national honor, there are many compensations in war. The armaments of Europe are often spoken of as a deadly weight upon the energies of the respective European countries. It is pointed out that the men are taken from their callings for service in the army in the best years of their life, the inference being that they lose a knowledge of their trade or profession, and lose the taste for work.

3

In the face of this we see Germany, which has brought its military system to the highest scientific perfection, rapidly becoming one of the great commercial and manufacturing nations of the world. Italy, also, has undoubtedly benefitted by her military system. One explanation of this apparent contradiction is that men are brought together from different sections of the country, acquire new tastes and ideas, and are impressed with the benefits of organization and the necessity for order and obedience. The country lad, who ordinarily would have no ideas above his plow and the routine of farmwork, becomes a broader man, and at the end of his military service is a more useful citizen.

Adequate strife of one kind and another, in the present order of nature and throughout nature, means progress. A few years ago Bluntschli, who presided at the Congress of International Law in Oxford, sent to Von Moltke a copy of the regulations which had

been drawn up by the congress for the conduct
of armies in time of war, their express object
being to lessen the hardships of war. In his
reply, Von Moltke said that he could express
but little sympathy with the movement.

He believed in war, not only as a necessity at
times, but in war for its own sake. He main-
tained that without it the nations would degenerate into money-loving and selfish people;
that war brought out the nobler traits in men,
and that to be ready to lay down one's life for
his country was an ultimate test of manhood.

Again, we are forced to recognize the benefits
of a successful war. Of these the most important relate to the political life of the nation,
internal as well as external. But when the
spirit of a healthy people is aroused by a
stirring national event the results are not
solely political. Such an event permeates the
whole world of mind and produces definite
results in industry as well. What explains the
surprising repair of waste often witnessed is

that the greatest factors in production are the character and trained habits of the people. These remain, even much of the machinery of production remains, after the most devastating war. The people and machinery can produce much more than they are ordinarily called upon to produce. When, therefore, the economic void which the waste of war has created sets all the people and all the machinery at work there follows a period of unusual prosperity, the effects of which are cumulative and lead to real development.

German unity with all its results for Germany, and for the world, could probably not have been attained in any other way than by a great war. It is likewise difficult to see how, without the frightful drama of the Civil War, America could have liberated the slave and demonstrated to the world that the Union was a thing of permanence and meant to fulfill the great destinies mapped out for it by the framers of its wonderful constitution. It has never known such a period of prosperity as that which followed the Civil War.

This is one side of the picture; the other has been too vividly painted by the brush of experience, and is too deeply burned in the hearts and brains of Americans to need description. By common consent, the dictates of humanity, and a sense of the awful suffering that accompanies war, clearly enjoin the avoidance of an unjust war. The true strength and manhood of an individual and of a nation are shown by their asserting their power only when a just occasion calls it forth. Is there such an occasion now in the controversy with England?

The Monroe Doctrine.

Our own authorities tell us that, from a standpoint of international law, we have nothing to stand upon. What we are about to do is to endeavor to insert into the international code a principle for which we have at times contended, but which has never yet been recognized. Is the principle justly interpreted by Secretary Olney? And were this so, is the present occasion a fitting one upon which to introduce it? And is the nation, to whom we are allied so strongly by ties of blood and tradition, the proper one upon which to make war in order to establish the principle?

In the minds of those who enunciated it, the Monroe doctrine clearly meant that no European government should be allowed to overturn the liberal governments of the western world in order to substitute for them a monarchical government, nor to seize upon territory there for purposes of colonization. Secretary Olney has so enlarged the scope of the doctrine that it embraces any territorial dispute between an American power and a European power. This is admittedly true, because he specifically disclaims any knowledge of the merits of this particular controversy. His language is: "It is not admitted, how-

ever, and, therefore, cannot be assumed, that
Great Britain is in fact usurping dominion
over Venezuelan territory."

England's Attitude Toward Arbitration.

Great Britain admits that the real owner-
ship of a portion of the territory is open to
question ; with respect to this portion she is
ready to submit to arbitration. In addition
to this, however, Venezuela claims territory
which Great Britain asserts to be hers abso-
lutely, and which has been settled by her
people.   Because of her aggressive policy, which
has really resulted in settling large regions of
the globe with a religious and a moral people,
and a people with traditions of political liberty,
she has but few friends amongst the nations,
and experience has taught her that she cannot
rely upon arbitration for fair decision of disputes to which she is a party. She is in the
position of a man, who, in a hostile land, has
had brought against him a claim for the pos-

session of property which he feels to be rightly
his and his children's, and is asked to submit
the claim to the judgment of a biased tribunal.
However much the members of an international
tribunal may be bent upon absolute fairness,
it cannot be denied that national prejudice will
unconsciously play an important part in their
decision.

It is admitted that the Monroe doctrine is
not a part of international law, and it would
appear from the above, moreover, that it is
questionable whether the doctrine is applicable
to the present dispute.   It remains to be considered whether England is the country of all
others with whom we should enter upon a war,
the justice of which is questionable, for the
establishment of a new principle as a part of
international law.

The English-speaking People.

The spread of the English-speaking people,
of whom we form an important part, is one of

the significant facts of the century. It has been pointed out that in 1700 there were 7,000,000 English-speaking people; at the beginning of the present century there were 20,000,000, and to-day we constitute a body of 115,000,000. What does this signify? Nothing less than the spread of liberal institutions, political freedom, humanity and enlightenment over a great portion of the world.

If we arrive at the conclusion that it is not to our interest to colonize, why should we block this movement, so important to civilization, by checking English colonization? Reflection will show us that we have many more ties with England, France, Germany or Italy than we have with the South American republics. They are building up everything that makes the modern world, science, art, philosophy, the principles of a broad humanity and the science of government.

The South American Republics.

What are the South American republics doing in all these walks? They are republics in name, but are they democracies in fact? The form of government has much to do with the happiness of a people, but the adoption of a good form cannot alone give the people a good government. Unless a government is so fortunate as to possess men enlightened and conscientious to a degree above their fellows (which is not often the case), it is apt to be good or bad, according as public opinion and the attention given to its expression insist or not upon its fulfilling its duties. The sense of civic duty, like everything else in the moral and intellectual world, depends upon environment. It is not uncommon to see a law passed which is quite in advance of public sentiment and which eventually educates public sentiment up to its high level; but generally it is unwise to count upon this. Laws will depend for their efficacy upon public support. If they do not reach the public conscience, they will do more harm than good. The harm is in their non-enforcement, which throws discredit upon law in general.

The South American republics are examples of admirable laws and institutions applied to people wholly unequal to the task of grasping their meaning. They may have other admirable qualities, but traditions of political liberty and a capacity for their exercise do not go with the Latin blood. It will require long years of practice to acquire them. We know how unstable their governments are, to what frequent revolutions they are subject, and how sadly they are found wanting when measured by the standard of international morality. To protect them against discipline at the hands of European powers means that we must ourselves be responsible for their actions, our readiness to do which Secretary Olney specifically and rightly disclaims.

England's Province.

England is charged with being grasping. In its foreign policy a nation should, above all, be a trustee—a guardian first of its people's honor, and then of their material interests. Considerations of general human sympathy and theoretic justice may play their part, but always subservient to the trusteeship. If a nation represents what is best in the world—and every nation must, of necessity, believe itself to represent the best either in its present state or future possibilities—it serves the interests of the world at large in extending its own possessions and influences by colonization. As commerce, in seeking its own ends, has brought about a revival of Roman law in Europe, and has supplanted savagery with civilization in many regions of the world, just so the self-seeking of a great nation unconsciously accomplishes a great good. England may have been unjust to us in our earlier days—even then it was

largely party and not the whole people—
but for many years she has had no other in-
tention than to treat us as nearest of kin and
regard us as her friend. Whilst our school
books, in treating of the Revolution, instil ani-
mosity toward England in the breast of the
majority of American children—and, unfor-
tunately, the mass of the people remain children in this respect—English children are
taught to respect the spirit of the American
Revolution, to honor the names of their own
great statesmen who advocated our cause at the
time, and to believe that our cause was just.
They regard the events which brought about
the American Revolution as a stupid mistake
on the part of the king and a clique who hap-
pened to be in power. The people, as a whole,
have no other than the most friendly regard
for us.

When the Monroe doctrine was framed, we
were so weak that the growth of a foreign
power on the American continent constituted a

menace to us. Truly, no sensible man regards
it as such to-day. Dispassioned observers must
admit that we are rapidly becoming the great
government of the world, and will soon be
forced to take our place at international coun-
cils, in spite of our home-keeping policy. We
are destined to be the peer of all in everything
that constitutes an enlightened people and an enlightened government. Jealousy should therefore be beneath us. Instead of courting war
with England, we should accept the invitation
extended by the members of the English House
of Commons to form a permanent treaty of
arbitration, and stand with her before the
world for all that we both represent in politics,
religion and morals. Such a union would be
the most powerful the world has ever seen, and
make for enlightened progress everywhere.

Our True Interests.

Moreover, if we are farseeing, we will not
block the extension of English colonization in

America. In this connection what French colonization did for England is significant. In India the French conquered an important region which eventually fell into the lap of England. France paved the way for England in Egypt. She was in the Mississippi Valley before England, and colonized Canada for her. Few doubt that our northern neighbor, by mere force of gravity, will in time become part of us, and the same would be the tendency with respect to English settlements elsewhere in America.

We might accomplish the same end by the establishment of a protectorate over the weak and more unstable South American countries, so that Anglo-Saxons would settle there. It is, however, to be questioned whether we have as yet sufficiently digested the heterogeneous immigration which has been coming to us, and whether our sinews are sufficiently formed to undertake such a disturbing task. Watch a stone which is thrown from a tall cliff, and you will see it drawn into the cliff before it reaches the ground below. The same law of gravitation will inevitably cause the nation to the north of us, allied by blood and tradition, to some day knock at the doors of the great republic for admission. If the natural process is too slow, we might take Canada by force. The objection to embodying Mexico, and Cuba likewise, on the ground that they are peopled by a race with traditions different from our own is not a valid one, because if they become part of us the emigration from the United States and from Anglo-Saxon countries would soon give us a preponderance of Anglo-Saxon blood in them. If, on the other hand, we decide that our policy for the present should not be that of expansion and colonization, why should we obstruct English expansion either in America or elsewhere? This involves discarding a portion of the Monroe doctrine, which, as has been pointed out, is really out of date, but leaves to us the nobler and more disinterested part of the doctrine, that which constitutes us the guardian and propagator of liberty in America.

To Sum Up:

First. The Monroe doctrine is not at present a part of the international law.

Second. The doctrine is not affected by the present controversy.

Third. To force ourselves into the controversy and to endeavor to establish the doctrine as a part of international law by a war with England is more than foolish, and would be a wrong to mankind.

Fourth. A part of the Monroe doctrine has lost its usefulness and should be discarded.

England and America stand for political progress in the modern world. All the governments in Continental Europe, except Russia and Turkey, are modelled either on the lines of the English government or American govern-

4

ment. We have together developed political
liberty, and to enter into war with one another
would most surely be a blow to civilization.

www.ingramcontent.com/pod-product-compliance
Lightning Source LLC
Chambersburg PA
CBHW030722110426
42739CB00030B/1168